IT'S NOW *OR NEVER*
OUR RACE TO SAVE **COLONEL PARKER'S** PLACE

AN OXVISION BOOK
BY BRIAN OXLEY

OXVISION
BOOKS

ISBN 978 1 938068 26 3

Library of Congress Control Number: 2017911569

© **2017 Oxvision Books**
All Rights Reserved. No part of this book or site may be reproduced or redistributed in any form or by any electronic or mechanical means, including information storage and retrieval systems, without permission in writing from Oxvision Media, LLC, except by a reviewer who may quote brief passages in a review.

Published by Oxvision Books
Oxvision Media, LLC, 4001 Tamiami Trail North, Suite 250, Naples, FL 34103

Find us at: **oxvisionmedia.com**

CONTRIBUTORS

AUTHORS
Brian Oxley

EDITORS
Devin Brown *&* Sally Oxley

PHOTOGRAPHERS *&* **FILM**
Kisa Kavass, Will Berry, Trevor George, Pony Ma, Lisa Roy, Sally Oxley, Dan Oxley, Chance Martin *&* Ron Keith

STORYTELLERS MUSEUM *&* **HIDEAWAY FARM**
storytellersmuseum.com

RON KEITH
Told me about the Colonel's house and worked on three renovations with me, showing me his art and heart for preserving history.

STEVE NORTH *&* **MARK NORTH**
Attorneys who owned the building for the last 20 years.

HISTORIC AUTO ATTRACTIONS
A museum dedicated to preserving history. *historicautoattractions.com*

GREG MCDONALD & LOANNE MILLER PARKER (*the Colonel's wife*)
Gave their support and knowledge.

TOMMY WORTHAM
Red Wortham's son, for providing important information, documents, record albums, and other memorabilia.

JEREMY HALL
Wash & Roll Car Wash, the new owner of the property who let us continue to dismantle the buildings and was very supportive.

DALE PAYNE & CREW
Sumner Roofing & Exteriors

JOHN SIMONSEN & CREW
Copper Creek Electric

WARREN TRUCKING

TENNESSEE CONTRACTOR RENTAL

HOME DEPOT RENTALS

WEST SIDE RENTAL & SALES

EAST HICKMAN MOBILE STORAGE

ARCHAEOLOGISTS

The team of "archaeologists" who helped to dismantle Colonel Parker's home, office, and the Fan Club building:

Anthony Peden	Anthony Brown	Dawson Pizzino
Ron (Rooster)	Isaac Vick	Bob Williams
Huston Hudson	Micah Vick	Terry Harris
Wayne Thomasson	Jesse Wickey	Brian Bailey
Ezra Schwartz	Gary White	Mitchel Stone
Jeff Warren	Ryan Dodd	
Eddie Warren	Billy Vaughn	
Richard Garner	Rodrigo Arauz	

Table of Contents

ABOUT THE COVER — xv

A PROMISE — xxv

INTRODUCTION — xxvii

CHAPTER 1 — The Great Red Wortham, Sam Phillips & a Young, Unknown Singer Named Elvis — 1

CHAPTER 2 — Gates, Doors, Security & Grand Closet — 11

CHAPTER 3 — Stone, Rock, Tiles & Bricks — 31

CHAPTER 4 — Basement, Trophy Room, Bar, Shower & Pillars — 61

CHAPTER 5 — Guest Bedroom Elvis Stayed in, Bathroom & Kitchen — 75

CHAPTER 6 — The Fan Club Building — 95

CHAPTER 7 — The Colonel's Cookhouse — 123

CHAPTER 8 — The Mighty Oak — 129

Table of Contents

CHAPTER 9	The King of Stumps	139
CHAPTER 10	Finding the Pond	149
CHAPTER 11	The Colonel & Elvis Served in the Military	157
CHAPTER 12	My Team & Friends	167
CHAPTER 13	Color	175
CHAPTER 14	Spiritual	185
CHAPTER 15	Conclusion	193

Thank you, Colonel Parker, for bringing Elvis Presley music and song to the world. The Colonel is receiving the Honorary Citizenship of Nashville award at his office in Madison, Tennessee. PHOTO: Given to us by the Nashville Public Library Metro Archives

DEDICATION

Chris Oxley, who has diligently and faithfully executed
and operated all my dreams, good and bad.
Without him I could never have been a dreamer.

Also, to the Elvis fans who have kept the stories of Elvis's kindness,
generosity, and love of God and gospel music alive for so many years.
This book is for you, the greatest fan club in the world that I have
joined in these later years of my life. Thank you, Elvis fans.

ABOUT THE COVER

The Elvis portrait on the book cover is an original
composition created by Wayne Brezinka,
an award-winning artist and illustrator.

Hailing from Nashville, Wayne uses paper, paint,
and found and re-purposed items to bring stories to life.
His distinctive multi-layered designs are unique historical
preservation documents.

Here is an index to some of the items from Colonel Parker's
complex in Madison that were used in the portrait.

IT'S NOW OR NEVER: OUR RACE TO SAVE COLONEL PARKER'S PLACE

ABOUT THE COVER

A Wires from the phone system that linked Colonel Parker to the world, his main tool for promoting his most famous client.

B Fan Club Membership Card showing the Fan Club Headquarters' famous address—P.O. Box 417, Madison, Tennessee.

C Original wood from the hallway in Madison that led to the Colonel's and Elvis's bedrooms.

D Stationery for the Colonel's All Star Shows with his trademark Conestoga wagon logo.

E Excerpts from "The Hound of Heaven," the classic poem by Francis Thompson with the lines: "My mangled youth lies dead beneath the heap" and "Lo, all things fly thee, for thou fliest Me!" Thompson and Elvis became addicted to drugs that initially were prescribed for them. Through all their trials, the great Pursuer's love for them never wavered.

IT'S NOW OR NEVER: OUR RACE TO SAVE COLONEL PARKER'S PLACE

ABOUT THE COVER

F The money clip found in Colonel Parker's closet, symbolizing his role in procuring profitable deals on behalf of Elvis through concerts, recordings, films, and merchandise.

G A vintage 45 RPM record produced at Sur-Speed Records, owned by Red Wortham whose tape of the Prisonaires led to Sam Phillips' recording "Just Walkin' in the Rain"—the record that led the young Elvis Presley to Sun Records.

H Dutch-themed wallpaper from the Fan Club building reflects the Colonel's memories of his home in Holland.

I A mid-century prescription bottle for narcotics, a reminder of Elvis's difficult battle with prescription drug abuse.

IT'S NOW OR NEVER: OUR RACE TO SAVE COLONEL PARKER'S PLACE

ABOUT THE COVER

J A cedar board from the closet that held Elvis's performance outfits rises up to a soaring Gothic arch reflecting Elvis's love for gospel music.

K An envelope from Hank Snow addressed to Colonel Tom Parker who represented Snow as well as Elvis.

L The elephant on an old Jumbo Peanuts Bag, reflecting the fact that the Colonel was an avid collector of elephant statues.

M A vintage Sun Records 45 record sleeve.

N A portion of the music and words to "How Great Thou Art"—the song that earned Elvis his first Grammy.

ABOUT THE COVER

Wayne Brezinka's original
artistic interpretation of Elvis
is on display at the
Storytellers Museum in Bon Aqua, Tennessee,
along with other materials from
Colonel Parker's complex.

Limited edition numbered prints are available for purchase.

A PROMISE

WHILE THE FIRST STEP IN SAVING COLONEL PARKER'S COMPLEX IS COMPLETE, THERE ARE MANY MORE TO COME.

As progress continues to be made on this project, here is our promise to you.

1. The finished project will include a provision so the poor will have access.

2. The finished project will be rich in Gospel music and its message of God's love and forgiveness. "Music and rhythm find their way into the secret places of the soul." –Plato

3. The finished project will acknowledge and proclaim the greatness of God that Elvis pointed to in the song "How Great Thou Art."

4. The finished project will help raise awareness of the destruction that is caused by opioid and prescription drug abuse.

INTRODUCTION

IT'S NOW OR NEVER: OUR RACE TO SAVE COLONEL PARKER'S PLACE

Brian Oxley

INTRODUCTION

On February 1, 2017, we set out on a journey that we thought would take two weeks.

Our goal was to save history—to remove and preserve the Elvis Fan Club building and Colonel Parker's home and office before they were torn down and replaced by a modern car wash. My inspiration came from Elvis's rendition of "How Great Thou Art" at his last concert just weeks before his death.

Our journey was a labor of love but also a response to anger, anger not just from the local community who did not want to lose an historic building, but also from Elvis's fans everywhere who were upset to learn that the place that held so many memories was going to be demolished.

Instead of 14 days, our journey took 120. After four months filled with many strange twists and unexpected turns, June 2nd became the last day that we would travel to the Colonel's property in Madison, Tennessee, to rescue what we could before it would be lost forever.

With the original section built in 1935, Colonel Parker's complex was made up of four separate buildings. His home featured period knotty-pine paneling and included a basement entertainment bar and bathrooms with pink, aqua, and black tiles. Elvis not only visited the Colonel's house on many occasions, he frequently slept there overnight. In the office he and the Colonel took care of business, and it was here that the famous call from Ed Sullivan came in. The Fan Club building was added behind the house in 1956 and had many of Elvis's gold records lining its ceiling.

Nearby stood the building referred to as the "White House."

As the story goes, when the Colonel didn't want to speak to someone, his wife would inform the caller that her husband was at the White House. And indeed the house is painted white.

Is it possible that the features Elvis saw when he stayed at the Colonel's property in Madison influenced his decision to buy Graceland in 1957? Both houses had four white pillars in front and metal bars over their windows and doors. Both had stone exteriors and shutters. Both had ponds. The bar in the basement at the Colonel's is a similar shape to the bar found in Elvis's basement room.

Behind the Fan Club building was a dilapidated bridge that led to another house which was full of memorabilia that had been sold to Graceland. When the trucks came, they filled a tractor-trailer, leaving behind what many people thought was an empty shell.

But in fact, it was not just a shell, but a treasure trove of history.

While this work of vision may have seemed extravagant in terms of the time and labor it took, our prayer is that in God's time the gain will be multiplied in the changed lives of people. What follows is the story—in pictures and words—of our attempt to save Colonel Parker's place in Madison, Tennessee, and to give the materials and memories a new home at the Storytellers Museum in Bon Aqua.

INTRODUCTION

Colonel Parker's Home & Office, Madison, Tennessee

CHAPTER 1

THE GREAT RED WORTHAM, SAM PHILLIPS & A YOUNG, UNKNOWN SINGER NAMED ELVIS

RED WORTHAM

The British poet T.S. Eliot once wrote, "The end of all our exploring will be to arrive where we started."

Eliot's statement certainly holds true for the world-famous Elvis Fan Club building.

After having stood for many years on Colonel Tom Parker's complex in Madison, Tennessee, the Fan Club building has found a new home at the Storytellers Museum in Bon Aqua—the place where the forces that led to the Elvis phenomenon were first put into motion.

Before it became the Storytellers Museum, the building that stands at the crossroads in Bon Aqua was owned by Johnny Cash. Johnny turned it into his Little Stage, a place to hold his legendary "Saturday Night in Hickman County" guitar pulls.

Before Johnny Cash owned the building, it was owned by another great from the music industry, Red Wortham, who made it into

a recording studio and the home of Sur-Speed Records.

And Red Wortham would play a key part in the discovery of Elvis Presley.

Born in Stewart County, Tennessee, in 1920, W.C. Wortham, or "Red" as he liked to be called, was a vital part of the Nashville area music scene during the 40s, 50s, and 60s and was known as a talented musician, a pioneering engineer, and an innovative producer.

Red began his music career as a jazz and big bands guitar player. He also played as a sideman in local groups that worked the hotel and

THE GREAT RED WORTHAM, SAM PHILLIPS & A YOUNG, UNKNOWN SINGER NAMED ELVIS

PHOTOGRAPH BY ALAN MESSER / WWW.ALANMESSER.COM

With my friend Tommy Wortham, Red Wortham's son.

nightclub circuit around Nashville. As country music began to grow, he was soon recording and producing full-time.

Red was an early master of audio engineering and helped create what has become known worldwide as the Nashville Sound. It has been said that he could do more with 2-track and 8-track recordings than most anyone in those early days of the industry.

Sur-Speed Records was just one of the many independent labels that Wortham founded. Others included the Bullet, Avenue, Silver City, Slam, Viking, and Gold Mine

Signatures of Johnny Cash & Red Wortham

labels. At that time, radio stations were cautious about playing too many records from the same label, so Red would create so-called custom labels that allowed him to get his artists more airtime.

But Red is best known for the role he played in the 1950s smash hit "Just Walkin' in the Rain" recorded by Johnnie Bragg and the Prisonaires.

The Prisonaires were five African-American male singers who were all inmates at the Tennessee State Penitentiary in Nashville. They were discovered when radio producer Joe Calloway heard them singing while he was preparing a news broadcast from the prison.

Red heard the broadcast and got permission to record the group at the prison. He sent a tape of the Prisonaires singing "Without You" to Jim Bulleit who sent it to Sam Phillips. Phillips arranged to have the group transported under armed guard to Memphis to record for his fledgling label Sun Records. A few weeks later, "Just Walkin' in the Rain" was released. It quickly sold 50,000 copies.

But the story does not end there.

Peter Guralnick, the author of *Last Train to Memphis,* claims that the Prisonaires' cover of "Just Walkin' in the Rain" was not just the song that put Sun Records on the map, it was the record that captured the attention of the young Elvis Presley.

It was the breakout success of "Just Walkin' in the Rain" that got Elvis thinking about Sun Records and its painstaking producer, Sam Phillips—a man who had staked his reputation on an unknown group and on a song whose melancholy notes Elvis heard over and over in his mind as well as on the radio.

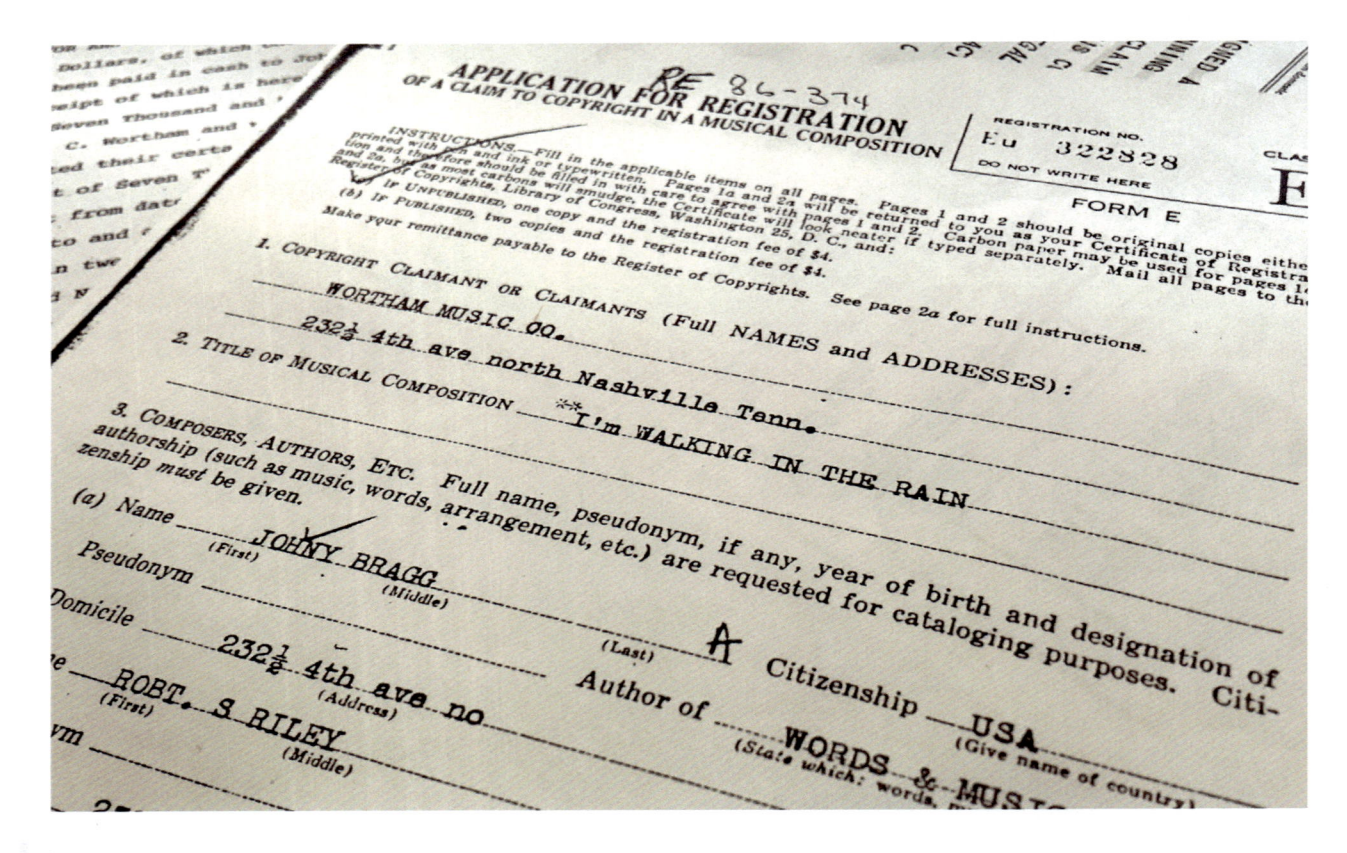

Application for registration of a claim to copyright
in a musical composition

But it was the modest, low-tech, acetate recording of the Prisonaires singing "Without You" from Red Wortham that got Sam Phillips first thinking about Elvis.

Guralnick explains how this happened:

> Its purity, its simplicity, above all the very amateurishness of the performance, put him in mind of the kid who had been stopping by….
>
> "What was his name?" he asked Marion, who seemed somewhat taken with the boy, a shy, insecure kid who had obviously never sung anywhere in his life.
>
> "Elvis Presley," Marion said and made the call.

After restorations at the Mama Cash House and Johnny Cash's Hideaway Farm, the Storytellers Museum was our third major project. And now four decades after Elvis's death, we had the unprecedented opportunity to save the Fan Club building—a task that feels more like a continuation of our previous endeavors than a new direction.

If the end of all our exploring is to arrive where we started, then the Fan Club building has found a fitting end to its journey in its new home at the Storytellers Museum, the place where the great Red Wortham also had his start.

And so the circle will be unbroken and finally complete.

CHAPTER 2

GATES, DOORS, SECURITY & GRAND CLOSET

GATES, DOORS, SECURITY & GRAND CLOSET

We left retirement in Florida for our fourth restoration project in Tennessee. Thank you, Sally, my wonderful (and patient!) wife.

IT'S NOW OR NEVER: OUR RACE TO SAVE COLONEL PARKER'S PLACE

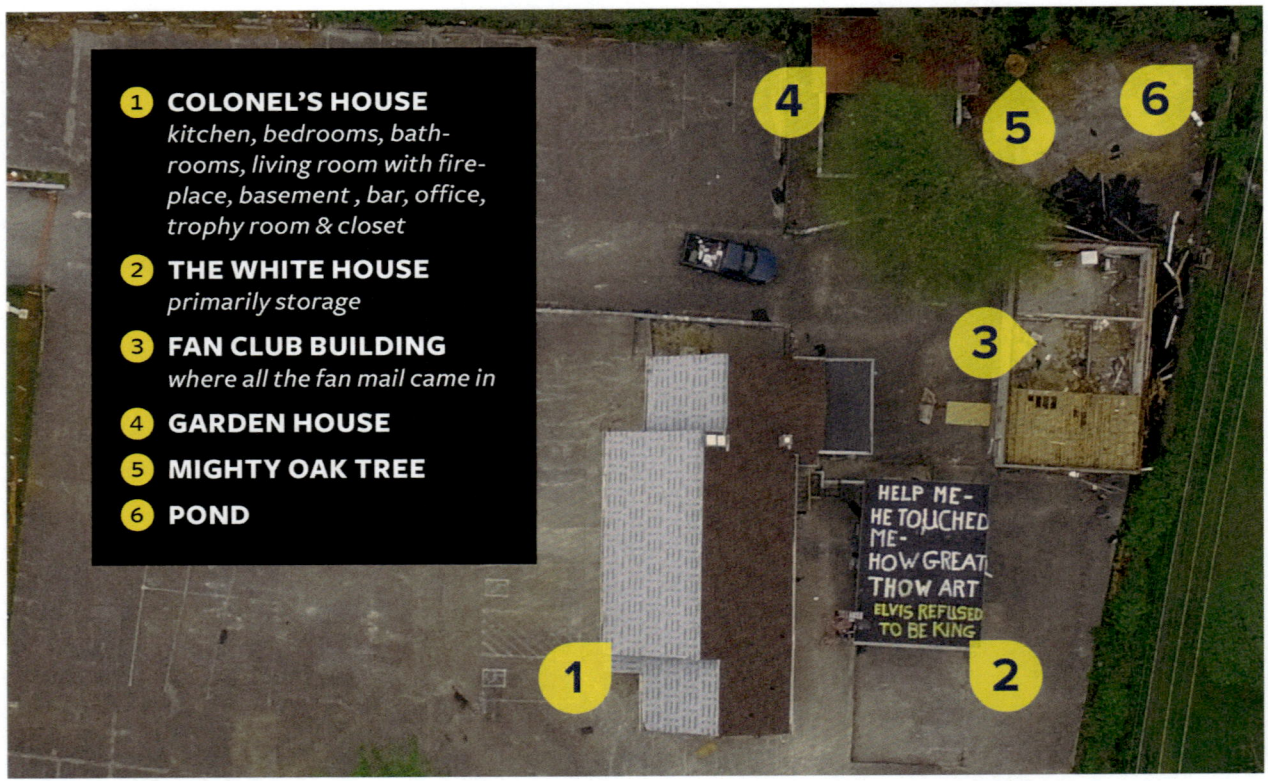

Elvis won three Grammys during his lifetime—all for sacred music: "How Great Thou Art" (1967), "He Touched Me" (1972), and for "How Great Thou Art—Recorded Live in Memphis" (1974).

GATES, DOORS, SECURITY & GRAND CLOSET

Our long journey to save Colonel Parker's place
began in winter and stretched into summer.

IT'S NOW OR NEVER: OUR RACE TO SAVE COLONEL PARKER'S PLACE

Elvis's first steps to becoming the world's greatest superstar began at these gates.

GATES, DOORS, SECURITY & GRAND CLOSET

To avoid being seen, Elvis came through the back entrance.

IT'S NOW OR NEVER: OUR RACE TO SAVE COLONEL PARKER'S PLACE

The handrails and steps Elvis used when he entered the Colonel's house through the back door are now at the farm.

GATES, DOORS, SECURITY & GRAND CLOSET

Here, each step is given a number before being carefully removed and stored.

The threshold that Elvis would cross as
he came in through the Colonel's back door.

GATES, DOORS, SECURITY & GRAND CLOSET

We pulled back the knotty-pine paneling in the Colonel's office and discovered an old garage door behind it which had been covered to expand his office space.

Redundant Security—double locks and barred glass were needed to protect the contents of Colonel Parker's home.

GATES, DOORS, SECURITY & GRAND CLOSET

Everyone who wanted Elvis had to go through Colonel Parker.
When Ed Sullivan called, this was the phone system that rang.

The Colonel's beautiful front entranceway with its ornate but solid security door.

GATES, DOORS, SECURITY & GRAND CLOSET

Cautiously lowering the front door before removal.

Walk through Colonel Parker's door to
a place filled with music and memories.

GATES, DOORS, SECURITY & GRAND CLOSET

The world's most iconic performance outfits hung here, including the famous gold lamé tuxedo made by Nudie Cohn for Elvis in 1956.

An interesting side story: Clara, a young girl who died of heart problems at the age of 11, always donated her best clothes when there was a clothing drive at her school. Hearing this, Judge North (who owned the property) decided to use Elvis's closets to store clothing for the poor. Clara is no longer with us, but her example lives on.

Elvis was always kind to the lonely and beaten down. He took pleasure in giving, often extravagantly, and would have loved Clara's story. Maybe they have already met in heaven. Wouldn't it be wonderful to listen in on their conversation?

CHAPTER 3

STONE, ROCK, TILES & BRICKS

STONE, ROCK, TILES & BRICKS

People often forget that Elvis's first Grammy was not for "Heartbreak Hotel" or "Blue Suede Shoes" but for the gospel album "How Great Thou Art."

The elegant living room and fireplace at the Colonel's house, much as it would have looked when Elvis came to visit.

STONE, ROCK, TILES & BRICKS

Here we see the living room fireplace with its decorative mantel removed revealing the brickwork underneath.

View from the attic looking down at the fireplace.

STONE, ROCK, TILES & BRICKS

One rock at a time—taking down the chimney.

All in a row—a sample of the bricks from Colonel Parker's house.

STONE, ROCK, TILES & BRICKS

IT'S NOW OR NEVER: OUR RACE TO SAVE COLONEL PARKER'S PLACE

Sliding bricks we salvaged down the ramp we constructed.

STONE, ROCK, TILES & BRICKS

Carefully catching bricks—to be labeled, stored, and one day reassembled.

Bricks from the living room fireplace, neatly arranged on the floor before being taken out to the trailer.

STONE, ROCK, TILES & BRICKS

Art from rubble, making "Stairway to Heaven."

IT'S NOW OR NEVER: OUR RACE TO SAVE COLONEL PARKER'S PLACE

Rocks salvaged from the exterior walls of the Colonel's house.

STONE, ROCK, TILES & BRICKS

An old rock that is bursting with seashells and looks like a dinosaur.

Delta—a beautiful stone shaped as a triangle, the Greek symbol for change.

STONE, ROCK, TILES & BRICKS

With Elvis as popular in Japan as he is back home, it is fitting that the salvaging project became a global effort that used Japanese Kubota equipment.

The great cement threshold from the main entrance to the house.

STONE, ROCK, TILES & BRICKS

The path leading to the front door. The Colonel built a concrete parking area that could accommodate buses and dozens of cars. Did he have future plans for a museum similar to the one at Graceland?

LEFT: Carefully removing a rock that is shaped like a skull, one of many unexpected discoveries. RIGHT: A rock that reminds me of the phantom of the opera.

STONE, ROCK, TILES & BRICKS

Behold, I stand at the door and knock. If anyone hears my voice and opens the door, I will come in to him and eat with him, and he with me. —Revelation 3:20

Piles of rocks and blocks exposed to the elements join nine large containers of materials from Madison now located at the farm.

STONE, ROCK, TILES & BRICKS

My father, a missionary to Japan, taught us long ago that something beautiful can rise again from fallen rocks.

Shingles are like individual freedoms—linked together they provide a strong shield for those who take shelter under them.

STONE, ROCK, TILES & BRICKS

Tiles flying from Colonel Parker's roof—a reminder of the music which sometimes seemed like a gift sent from heaven to touch our souls.

The tiles from Colonel Parker's bathroom—a puzzle for grown-ups!

STONE, ROCK, TILES & BRICKS

A photo in Japan of a pile of rubble with the Japanese characters "Warning: Falling rocks." Nothing man builds will last, only our souls. Colonel Parker's home will one day crumble. We have preserved as much as we can, but even that will go up in ashes someday.

A once important building facing the wrecking ball—a reminder to us all.

CHAPTER 4

BASEMENT, TROPHY ROOM, BAR, SHOWER & PILLARS

BASEMENT, TROPHY ROOM, BAR, SHOWER & PILLARS

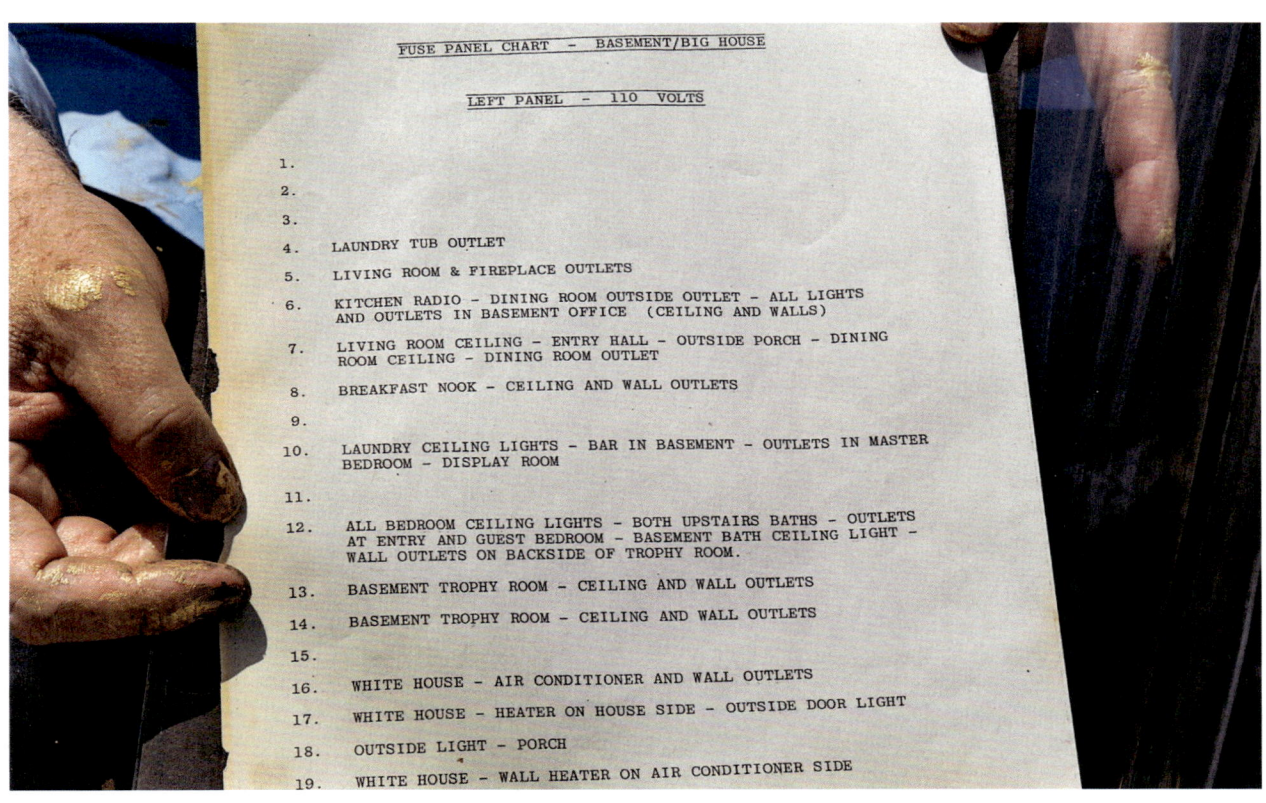

The list of names the Colonel gave to various places on the complex—as seen in these labels from the electric panel.

IT'S NOW OR NEVER: OUR RACE TO SAVE COLONEL PARKER'S PLACE

The Colonel's bar in the basement—an intimate place where he and Elvis could talk and have a drink.

BASEMENT, TROPHY ROOM, BAR, SHOWER & PILLARS

The poles are like those from a carousel—the Colonel always a carnie. These poles were next to the bar in the basement of Colonel Parker's home. Now safely at the farm, waiting for a home.

Taking down the basement ceiling.

BASEMENT, TROPHY ROOM, BAR, SHOWER & PILLARS

The last five pillars from the basement. All the pillars have been preserved. Pillars have traditionally been symbols of strength.

The basement shower being taken away one piece at a time.

BASEMENT, TROPHY ROOM, BAR, SHOWER & PILLARS

A collection of the objects found at the Colonel's house—razors and a brush from the medicine cabinet in the bedroom Elvis used as well as an assortment of keys and other items.

Over a hundred old razor blades—many of which Elvis might have used—were found in the walls behind the bathroom vanities.

BASEMENT, TROPHY ROOM, BAR, SHOWER & PILLARS

Razor blades, having fallen in from the small slots in the medicine cabinets behind the mirrors, were forgotten and never to be retrieved, until now.

A CHANCE MEETING AT THE COLONEL'S OFFICE

David McCormick, who initially worked at and is now the owner of Ernest Tubb Record Shop, tells the story of a visit that he and Charles Mosley, Tubb's accountant, made to Colonel Parker's office.

As a young man, David had been to the studio where Elvis was recording his 1968 gospel album and was briefly introduced to him. Sometime later he and Mr. Mosley were at Colonel Parker's, and David happened to cross paths with Elvis again.

"Elvis didn't know me from Adam, of course. But when I reintroduced myself and told him Ernest Tubb Record Shop, he said, 'Oh, I remember, Beasley Smith and you came down to the recording studio.'

"I wouldn't have thought he'd have even remembered that day. He was always so very kind. It was a real thrill for me to get to be around him for the short time that I was.

"In 1954, Elvis sang on 'The Grand Ole Opry' and was not very well received. Mr. Tubb brought Elvis over to the Midnight Jamboree afterwards and he sang two songs on the show that night. Mr. Tubb later got a letter from Elvis thanking him for saving his weekend in Nashville.

"Theirs was a friendship that lasted through the years. Every February we would get a huge box of chocolates at the record shop. They were delivered every February 9th—Mr. Tubb's birthday. He would always get that box of chocolates from Elvis."

BASEITEMENT, TROPHY ROOM, BAR, SHOWER & PILLARS

Ernest Tubb Record Shop, Nashville, Tennessee

CHAPTER 5

GUEST BEDROOM ELVIS STAYED IN, BATHROOM & KITCHEN

GUEST BEDROOM ELVIS STAYED IN, BATHROOM & KITCHEN

ELVIS SLEPT HERE! Wood paneling lined the walls and ceiling of the second bedroom at the Colonel's home. Each panel has been carefully labeled for future reconstruction.

The view looking up from the basement toward the floor of the Elvis bedroom. Small holes were drilled to let light through for photographing.

GUEST BEDROOM ELVIS STAYED IN, BATHROOM & KITCHEN

Standing in the guest bedroom—everything has been removed and transported to the farm, anticipating the rebuilding of this room formerly used by Elvis.

Open and empty, the bedroom Elvis used is now a visual symbol of the great gospel song "I'll Fly Away."

GUEST BEDROOM ELVIS STAYED IN, BATHROOM & KITCHEN

Marbles found in the ductwork—possibly lost down the vent in the Elvis bedroom.

IT'S NOW OR NEVER: OUR RACE TO SAVE COLONEL PARKER'S PLACE

Rex Humbard and his wife met with Elvis backstage in Las Vegas. Mrs. Humbard told Elvis she was praying he might become a bell sheep for God.

GUEST BEDROOM ELVIS STAYED IN, BATHROOM & KITCHEN

As she explained to him: "In the Holy Land, they put a bell on one sheep and when it moves all the rest of the flock moves with him. If you fully dedicated your life to God you could lead millions of people into the kingdom of the Lord."

IT'S NOW OR NEVER: OUR RACE TO SAVE COLONEL PARKER'S PLACE

Carrying out the kitchen cabinet in one piece to not disturb the tile. Read the paraphrased message (on the following pages) of a person invited to sit in the kitchen long ago.

MEMORIES OF A VISIT TO COLONEL PARKER'S HOUSE

The Colonel's house will soon be gone, but not the memories.

While attending Madison High, I worked at the old Madison Square Esso for five years where I met a lot of fun and interesting people. But looking back, I think the nicest person I ever met was Elvis.

I don't think Mr. Parker was even a real colonel, but he was adamant that others address him as such. I had no problem with that and afforded him the respect adults were given in those days, and he seemed to like that. I also knew that the Lincoln Continental Mark II he drove was ultra-rare and cost a small fortune, and I always made it a point to tell the Colonel how much I liked it. Consequently, I was the only one allowed to gas her up, check under the hood, or put air in the tires. And he trusted only me when he brought her in for a wash and interior cleaning. I knew he was in the music business and lived in the stone house down from St. Joseph's. He'd sometimes ask what I thought about a particular group or singer. One Saturday near the end of September 1964, he asked if I liked Elvis.

"Shoot yeah, Colonel Parker," I said. "I love Elvis!"

"Okay, next time he's in town, I'll have you over," the Colonel replied.

I thought he'd been joking and was quite surprised when about a month later he made good on his promise.

I drove through the open gates and pulled my '54 Super 88 next to the gorgeous red and white '63 T-Bird convertible and the shiny new '64 Coupe de Ville. I was led down the pine-paneled hallway covered with pictures and awards to the kitchen. There sitting at the table was Elvis. He was drinking a Coke from one of the little green, seven-ounce bottles. I called him Mr. Presley, but he was quick to note that he was only 29 and appreciated my manners but he'd rather I just call him Elvis.

In the several hours that followed, we talked about everything from motorcycles and cars, to his time in the army, to how we both hated school. I remember him saying that he always looked forward to coming to Madison and wouldn't mind living here someday. The one thing I couldn't understand was his telling me that he started out as a truck driver and mechanic and most days wished he'd stuck with that. That was hard for a 16-year-old kid to grasp and went right over my head.

We probably could have gone on forever had not the Colonel poked his head through the arched doorway and reminded us that RCA was waiting. Elvis thanked me for spending my Saturday morning with him and told me he would be really mad if he found out I was in Memphis and didn't call. I shook his hand and thanked him for having me over, and I told him to stop by the Esso station next time he was in town.

I didn't get my picture taken with Elvis, nor did I get his autograph. But what I did take away was an enduring memory of a wonderful human being and another great memory of growing up in Madison.

—by Jerry Malone

GUEST BEDROOM ELVIS STAYED IN, BATHROOM & KITCHEN

As Elvis ate his banana and peanut butter sandwich, he could look at the beautiful view from Colonel Parker's kitchen window.

The Colonel's bathroom with its unique wall tiles and floor tiles.

GUEST BEDROOM ELVIS STAYED IN, BATHROOM & KITCHEN

The stylish guest bathroom that was used by Elvis when he stayed overnight at the Colonel's house.

Two hound dogs sitting on the tub that was used by Elvis.

GUEST BEDROOM ELVIS STAYED IN, BATHROOM & KITCHEN

These floor tiles from the guest bathroom were particularly reluctant to say goodbye to their old home. Checkered floor tiles from the upstairs bathrooms used by the Colonel, Elvis, and other guests.

A hound dog inspects the tiles from the Colonel's guest bathroom and finds they ain't nothing but bath tiles!

CHAPTER 6

THE FAN CLUB BUILDING

The Fan Club building—the people's house. What did the fans love about Elvis? I believe it was the man—his kindness and humility in greatness and his refusal to usurp the kingship of Jesus.

A Dutch-themed design located across from the mail-sorting table in the Fan Club building reflects the Colonel's memories of Holland and its beauty.

Looking out the door of the Fan Club building at the trailer—its temporary home and rescuer.

Always thankful—always there.

THE FAN CLUB BUILDING

The Fan Club building's power system. It could be said that the real energy that powered this building did not come from the electric wires held up by this slender pole, but from the fans who kept, and continue to keep, the stories and memories alive.

IT'S NOW OR NEVER: OUR RACE TO SAVE COLONEL PARKER'S PLACE

The sorting table, over 30 feet long, was found in the mailroom. This was where all the fan mail came in and was organized. This table is now preserved for history and Elvis fans everywhere.

THE FAN CLUB BUILDING

Looking up at the beautiful, paneled ceiling in the Fan Club building where Elvis's gold records were hung.

IT'S NOW OR NEVER: OUR RACE TO SAVE COLONEL PARKER'S PLACE

A new geometry—Columbus and Lindbergh used celestial navigation, here we use knot navigation to locate where Elvis and the Colonel sat in their iconic photo.

THE FAN CLUB BUILDING

The iconic 1950's photo of Elvis and the Colonel showing the knotty-pine paneling in the Fan Club and Elvis's favorite jacket.

The knotty-pine paneling from the corner in the Fan Club building where Elvis and Colonel Parker took the famous picture will be reassembled exactly like it was.

THE FAN CLUB BUILDING

Preparing to take down the walls of the Fan Club building—a final farewell to a much-loved structure.

The unpretentious bathroom in the Fan Club building.

THE FAN CLUB BUILDING

The start of a new chapter—taking down the first piece of the Fan Club wall.

A buttermilk carton is discovered—left behind many years ago when the Fan Club building was built.

THE FAN CLUB BUILDING

Mail addressed to Colonel Parker found in the blocks.

Colonel Parker was also Hank Snow's manager. This vintage poster from the concert in Lincoln, Nebraska, was the grand prize of the objects we discovered in the blocks of the Fan Club building.

Envelopes found in the cavities of the blocks of the Fan Club building.

Another day of hunting for treasure in the walls of the Fan Club building.

THE FAN CLUB BUILDING

Layers of history—nails from another era pulled from the Fan Club building indicate that the wood had come from an earlier project and is now headed to be used once more.

IT'S NOW OR NEVER: OUR RACE TO SAVE COLONEL PARKER'S PLACE

Walking through the rubble of the Fan Club building.

THE FAN CLUB BUILDING

A rough-cut memorial to Elvis and the Colonel
ready to be taken out to the farm.

IT'S NOW OR NEVER: OUR RACE TO SAVE COLONEL PARKER'S PLACE

Flags from all over the world fly above the spot where the Fan Club building stood—colorful reminders of the Elvis fans who can be found in every country on Earth.

THE FAN CLUB BUILDING

The U.S. flag flys bravely over the Fan Club building as more rocks are brought down from the Colonel's house. A sign on the window shows where the Colonel had his lovely knotty-pine office, a room which originally had been the garage.

The cement floor of the Colonel's office in the Fan Club building where the Colonel and Elvis sat for this photo.

CHAPTER 7

THE COLONEL'S COOKHOUSE

THE COLONEL'S COOKHOUSE

The Colonel's Cookhouse out back—where barbecue was king.

Colonel Parker's Cookhouse next to the mighty oak tree.

"Enterprise No 1, Out Door Cook, Phillips A Buttorff, Nashville Tenn."

CHAPTER 8

THE MIGHTY OAK

On February 1st, we started our journey. What we initially thought was a two-week journey to preserve history—the Elvis Fan Club building and Colonel Parker's home and office—has now extended to 120 days. We thought May 26th would be our final day, but with many twists and turns on our journey, June 2nd became the final day.

Cold and unclean, the gray concrete covers the once green forest floor. The lonely acorns once fell on warm, welcoming ground, but now tumble as the wind blows them across the cold, hard surface.

THE MIGHTY OAK

How could an acorn grow to be such a mighty oak tree?

IT'S NOW OR NEVER: OUR RACE TO SAVE COLONEL PARKER'S PLACE

THE MIGHTY OAK

Then we saw something up high in the old oak tree—an unmistakable hand with five fingers and a pierced palm. Art formed far above the ground—coincidence?

Let your imagination soar. Do you see what I see—the Million Dollar Quartet: Johnny Cash and Carl Perkins at the top leaning against each other as friends, while Jerry Lee Lewis and Elvis took different paths, yet all connected together by a heart pumping the blood and nutrition to the arteries of the music industry? The thick bark speaks to me of the hard life each one lived. They paid the price for our great pleasure.

If this tree could see, think of what it might have seen—the bloody Civil War, farmers clearing forests to grow food, then cutting trees to build homes. Which tree would be next? We were left with the task of cutting the doomed tree. It would be cut down to make way for the car wash. So we cut the tree in tears, but we would create a beautiful monument for people to remember the great oak tree. A few months later I started thinking about the stump, which spent close to 300 years in the dark, doing its duty, providing a foundation for the mighty oak. The roots never saw the sunset, nor did it see Elvis looking up at it. So on what we thought was the final day, May 26th, we would release the stump from its grave.

THE MIGHTY OAK

Do you see an elephant? Colonel Parker's favorite animal, he always wanted the trunk to be pointing up. He had a large collection of elephant art and statues.

IT'S NOW OR NEVER: OUR RACE TO SAVE COLONEL PARKER'S PLACE

THE MIGHTY OAK

The Colonel, originally from Holland, was surrounded by mystery of how he landed in the U.S.

Nevertheless, you could see evidence of his love for Holland in wallpaper that covered shelving in the Fan Club building. Prince Bernhard of Holland also loved elephants. He founded and became president of the Prince Bernhard Nature Fund.

CHAPTER 9

THE KING OF STUMPS

THE KING OF STUMPS

Relaxing on the stump during the early stages of its removal.

The shadow came, and then it disappeared.

THE KING OF STUMPS

Determined to remove the stump.

The battle to unlock the stump from the ground took 12 hours. We shook and rocked the stump for hours on end. Finally, the steel machine, man's tool for modernization, ripped the roots of the tree.

THE KING OF STUMPS

The large dump truck could barely hold the stump. Finally, yielding to the power of the machine, the task was completed. The stump would make its home at the Hideaway Farm.

Where the tree stump once stood.

CHAPTER 10

FINDING THE POND

So this led to the final extension. We would come back on June 2nd and would pull back the old gray concrete slab that covered the property next to the Fan Club building.

Then it happened, at the farthest corner, next to an old rock wall, two feet below the concrete slab we found a brick wall covered with waterproof material. On June 2nd, our final day, we found the pond where Elvis was known to have fed the fish.

IT'S NOW OR NEVER: OUR RACE TO SAVE COLONEL PARKER'S PLACE

As we dug out the root we saw a lower level of concrete—a different color—bricks lined with waterproof lining, the first indication that the pond we were looking for was nearby.

The Colonel's pond was located at the base of this wall in the back corner of the complex behind the other buildings.

The corner piece from the pond wall still intact.

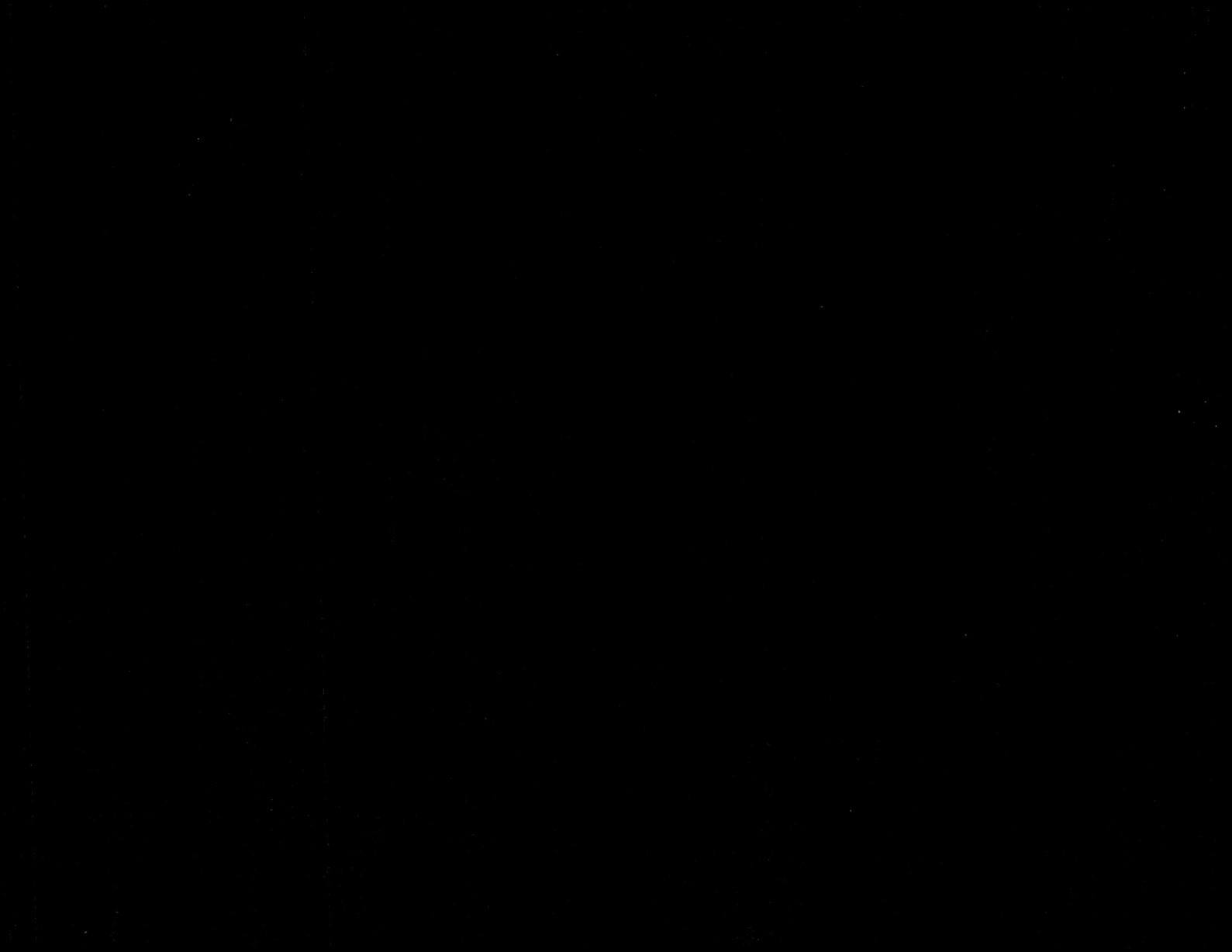

CHAPTER 11

THE COLONEL & ELVIS SERVED IN THE MILITARY

THE COLONEL & ELVIS SERVED IN THE MILITARY

A tattered flag holds in the midst of the rubble.

IT'S NOW OR NEVER: OUR RACE TO SAVE COLONEL PARKER'S PLACE

Never forget 9/11.

THE COLONEL & ELVIS SERVED IN THE MILITARY

An inspiration to all—the Stars and Stripes of the U.S. flag once flew high above the defeated nation of Japan. In partnership with the U.S. occupation forces, the nation of Japan rose from the ashes.

IT'S NOW OR NEVER: OUR RACE TO SAVE COLONEL PARKER'S PLACE

A tribute to all the men and women
who served in uniform—past, present, and future.

THE COLONEL & ELVIS SERVED IN THE MILITARY

A U.S. marine, my father oversaw the Japanese election.
Yes, he was a part of the Greatest Generation.

Hand to hand—carefully passing down sections of the chimney.

THE COLONEL & ELVIS SERVED IN THE MILITARY

Elvis's second Grammy "He Touched Me."

CHAPTER 12

MY TEAM & FRIENDS

MY TEAM & FRIENDS

My brother Dan and his wife Donna.

My team—I'm proud of each one.

MY TEAM & FRIENDS

Climbing onto the powerful backhoe that did so much work for us.

Whatever I do and wherever I go, my daughters are always on my mind.
Elvis, a father himself, knew the feeling of constant care a parent has.

CHAPTER 13

COLOR

COLOR

The colors of a Blue Hawaii beach found during the reclamation.

Thirteen different shades of blue—which was the Colonel's favorite color.

COLOR

The view into the living room from the front porch, where we painted and celebrated the Colonel's favorite color and Elvis's greatest song.

Bricks of a different color—all used in the construction of Colonel Parker's complex.

COLOR

Carl Perkins' blue suede shoes—the shoes that set Tom Parker dancing.

A discarded matchbox we came across,
a dirt-covered treasure from long ago.

CHAPTER 14

SPIRITUAL

SPIRITUAL

A rock in the shape of a heart, a token of the love shared by Elvis and his fans.

So now faith, hope, and love abide, these three; but the greatest of these is love. —I Corinthians 13:13

My 92-year-old mother and her first graffiti experience.

SPIRITUAL

I reminded my mother that long ago in the small village of Hitoyoshi, Japan, she made me wear Japanese graffiti on my back, telling our Japanese neighbors not to feed me candy because of stomach problems. This was not a cool experience.

Everything Must Be Sold. Even Christ was sold for 30 pieces of silver.

CHAPTER 15

CONCLUSION

CONCLUSION

Our last day. Still loving each other.

Having reached the end of this long and winding road, I look back and ask myself if it was worth all the time and effort. Was it really worth it?

My answer is "Absolutely!"

We experienced so many thrilling moments when our hard work led to unexpected discoveries—such as the day we found the envelopes preserved in the cavities of the cinder blocks, or the very last day when we dug out the root of the stump, which led to our finding the pond.

I think of when we came across what could have been Elvis's marbles in the ductwork or when we found a beautiful monument high up in the tree that looked like the hand of God, or an elephant, or maybe even the Million Dollar Quartet.

But of all the blessings associated with this project, the one that touched my heart the most was the kindness of the team I worked with—truly a band of brothers. I'll never forget their enthusiasm for what we were trying to accomplish. I am also thankful for the love and support of my wife who provided us with water, food, and supplies.

I remember the day I climbed up the ladder and wanted to get out on the roof. Perhaps noticing the fact that I am somewhat overweight and approaching 70, my team insisted on putting "steps" on top so that I could climb more easily. Then when I was ready to come down, they brought the big bucket and gently helped me into it. I had climbed up, but I got to ride down!

Every time I was sitting on the ground and trying to get up, there was always a hand reaching down to help me. Never having been in war, I felt a little of what it must

CONCLUSION

IT'S NOW OR NEVER: OUR RACE TO SAVE COLONEL PARKER'S PLACE

CONCLUSION

have been like as I experienced the camaraderie of just hanging out with my team—flesh and blood.

As the days stretched into weeks, I also developed a real appreciation for Elvis and the Colonel and all they did to please the fans. We were working too hard and were often very tired and had little time to waste—factors which made me reflect on the vulnerabilities that the Colonel and Elvis experienced in their own lives. Most days we were a weary band of brothers with no time to focus on anyone else's faults.

Now and then elderly people would stop by, sometimes with sadness in their eyes as they told us they wished the Colonel's complex could have remained as it was. We tried to talk to everyone who came and sometimes would give them a little piece from the house to take with them. At least we were able to offer the consolation of telling them it would be preserved somewhere else.

On June 23rd, we headed for Madison for the last time, ready to say farewell to this property that had made such a place in our hearts and to film the final demolition of Colonel Parker's home and office.

As we approached, we saw a huge machine out in front, but the house and the other buildings were gone, or nearly so. I was shocked and saddened not to have been there to see the last moments of the house. Not being able to say goodbye almost felt like being with a close friend in the hospital for weeks, then stepping out briefly to go to the cafeteria and missing the very end.

Later, the operator of the great machine showed up and told me that anticipating poor weather, he had decided to take it down the day before. So this is what we saw—just the final wall waiting to come down, like the face of a beast in agony over its coming destruction.

The operator told us that it took only 10 minutes to bring down what we had left behind. A stark contrast to the 120 days it took to preserve what we could of the property.

The operator was kind enough to take down the remaining wall—the beast—to complete its mission. After the wall was demolished, what was left of the house imploded into the basement.

Through this whole experience, we had a chance to focus on Elvis's Grammy-award winning song "How Great Thou Art." As our days in Madison stretched on to weeks, it seemed like the song was everywhere—in the people we met, in His creation, and in the old oak tree that was so beautiful.

In the end, we moved over 100 tons of material. Each bit had come from God. The beautiful stones from the exterior of the house. The simple clay bricks, each with its own color and character. The knotty-pine paneling with no two boards alike, like fingerprints that told us exactly where the Colonel and Elvis had sat. So many different materials—wood, clay, brick, stone, glass, and tile. So many different colors. All part of God's amazing creation. How great He is!

O wonderful, wonderful and most wonderful, wonderful! And yet again wonderful....

—William Shakespeare

Well, it's not surprising to me that Elvis loved gospel songs. And of all of them, his favorite was "The Sweet By and By." Elvis knew where he was going in the sweet

CONCLUSION

201

IT'S NOW OR NEVER: OUR RACE TO SAVE COLONEL PARKER'S PLACE

CONCLUSION

by and by. He knew who was King. And he knew it wasn't him.

Here's to the next chapter in the life of the materials we moved and the memories we preserved!

The universe resounds with the joyful cry, I am!
—Alexander Scriabin

Made in the USA
Lexington, KY
24 August 2017